Nature Upclose

An Earthworm's Life

Written and Illustrated by John Himmelman

Children's Press®
A Division of Scholastic Inc.
New York Toronto London Auckland Sydney
Mexico City New Delhi Hong Kong
Danbury, Connecticut

For Bill Yule,
May your meadows be filled
with worms!

Library of Congress Cataloging-in-Publication Data

Himmelman, John
A earthworm's life / written and illustrated by John Himmelman.
    p. cm. — (Nature upclose)
    Summary: Describes, in simple text and illustrations, the
daily activities and life cycle of the earthworm.
    ISBN 0-516-21164-1 (lib. bdg.)   0-516-26535-0 (pbk.)
    1. Earthworms—Juvenile literature. 2. Earthworms—Life
cycles—Juvenile literature. [1. Earthworms.] I. Title
QL391.A6 H56 2000
592'.64—dc21   99-045780
                                    CIP

Earthworm
Lumbricus terrestris

Earthworms spend most of their lives underground. They tunnel through the soil, eating it as they go. They also eat dead leaves.

After plants and soil pass through an earthworm's body, the earthworm leaves the waste materials in small piles near the entrance to its tunnel. These piles are called castings. Castings contain nutrients and help plants grow. An earthworm's tunnels allow air into the soil, so farmers and gardeners are happy to have earthworms around.

Have you ever noticed earthworms on a street or sidewalk after a heavy rain? They have been flooded out of their tunnels and are looking for a drier place to dig a new burrow.

There is no such thing as a male earthworm or a female earthworm. Every earthworm is a hermaphrodite (her MA fro dyt). Sometimes it acts like a male and sometimes it acts like a female. All earthworms can lay eggs.

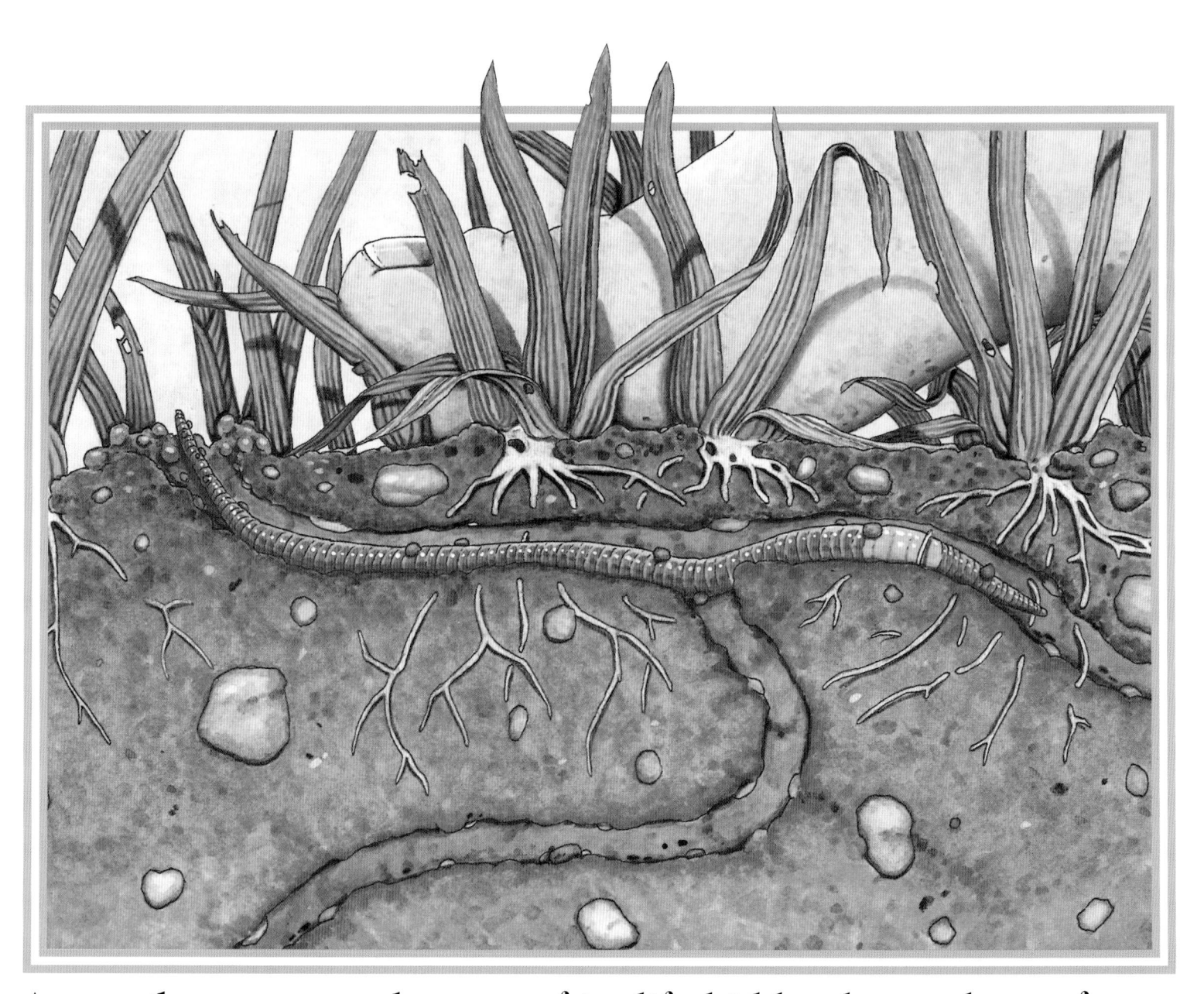

An earthworm spends most of its life hidden beneath our feet.

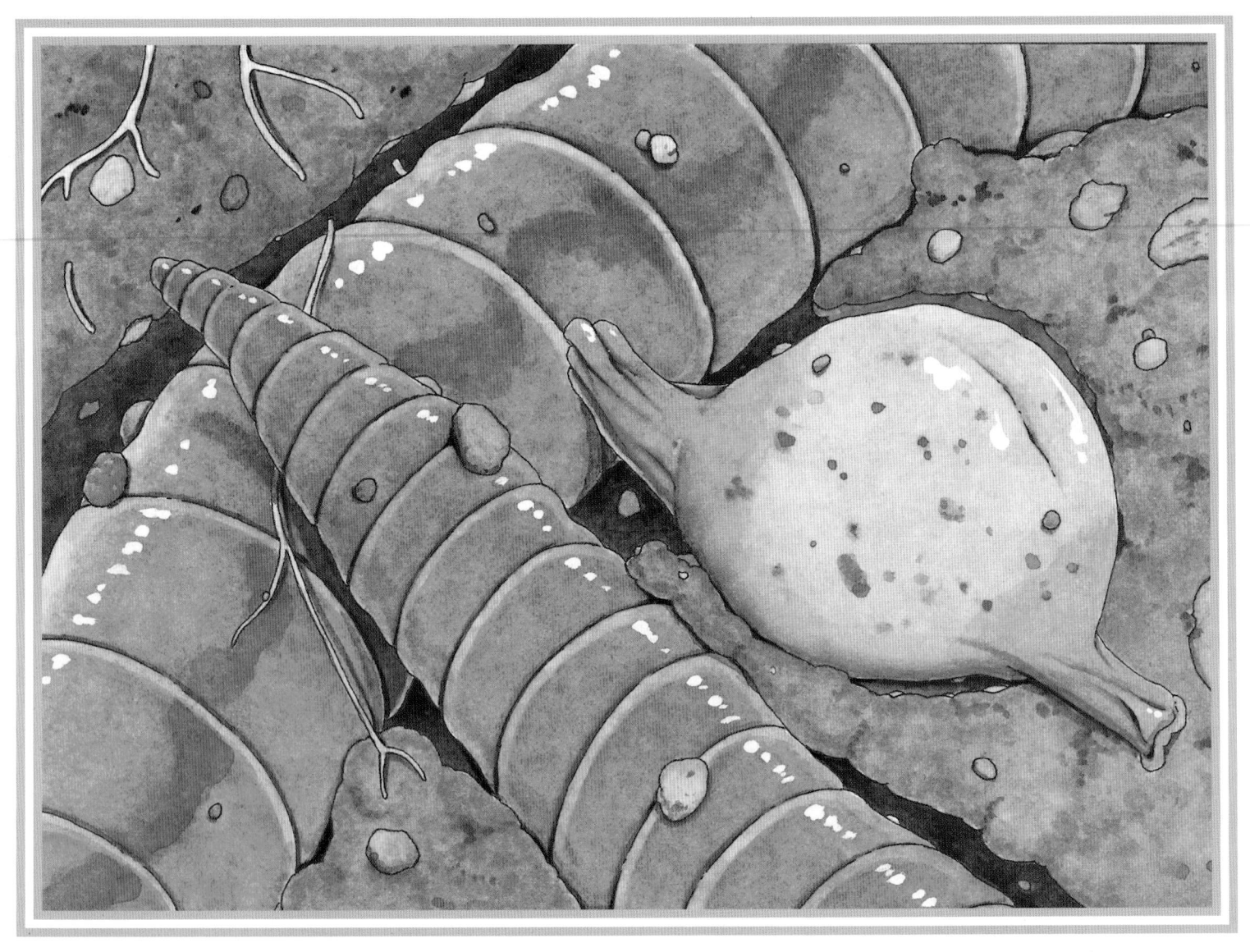

In spring, an adult earthworm leaves its *egg case* in an underground *burrow*.

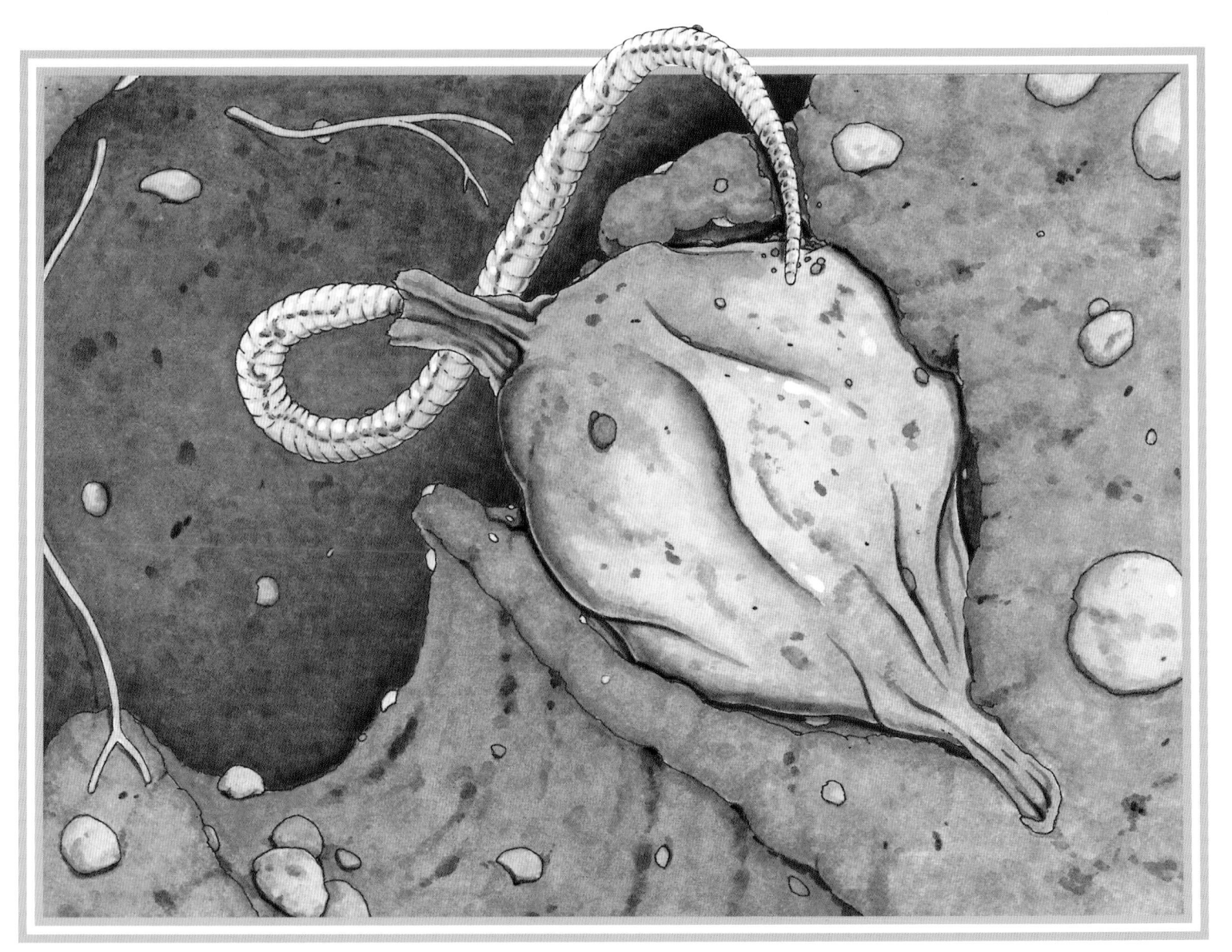

Two months later, a baby earthworm hatches from its egg. It crawls out of the egg case.

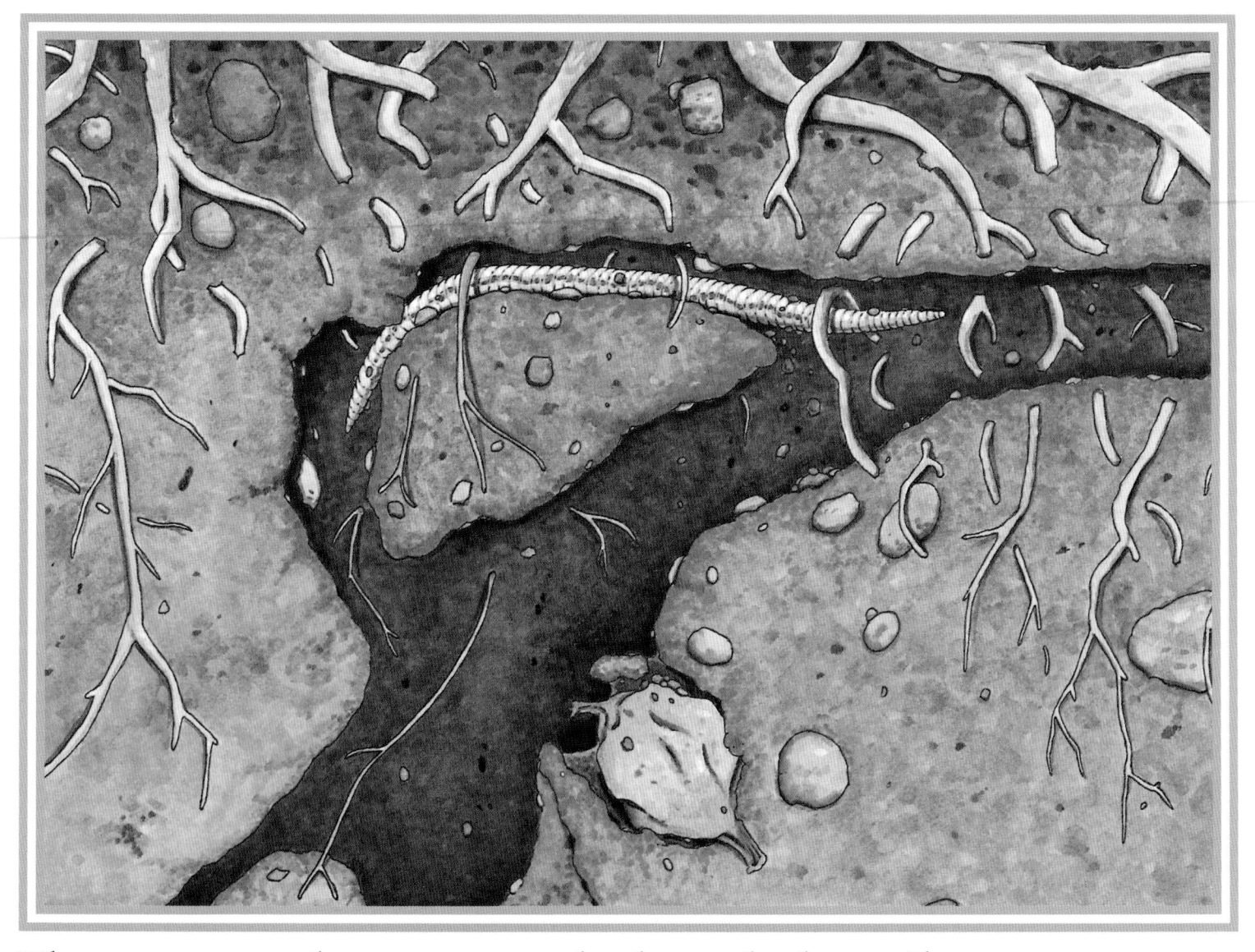

The young earthworm tunnels through the *soil.*

At night, it feeds on dead leaves.

Sometimes the earthworm eats soil.

The soil goes through the earthworm's body. It comes out as a pile of round balls called *castings.*

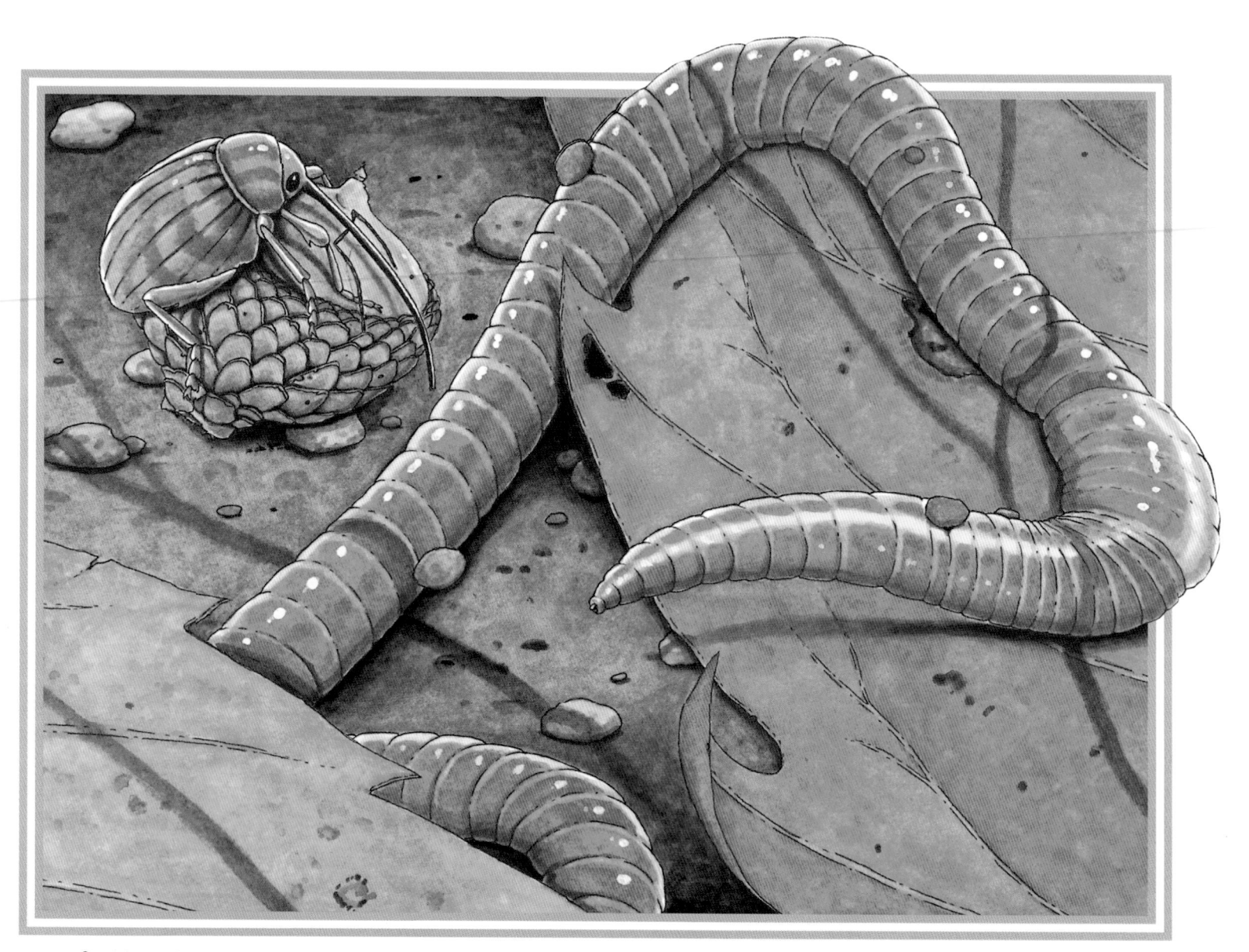

By fall, the earthworm is nearly full grown.

It pulls dead plants into its burrow.

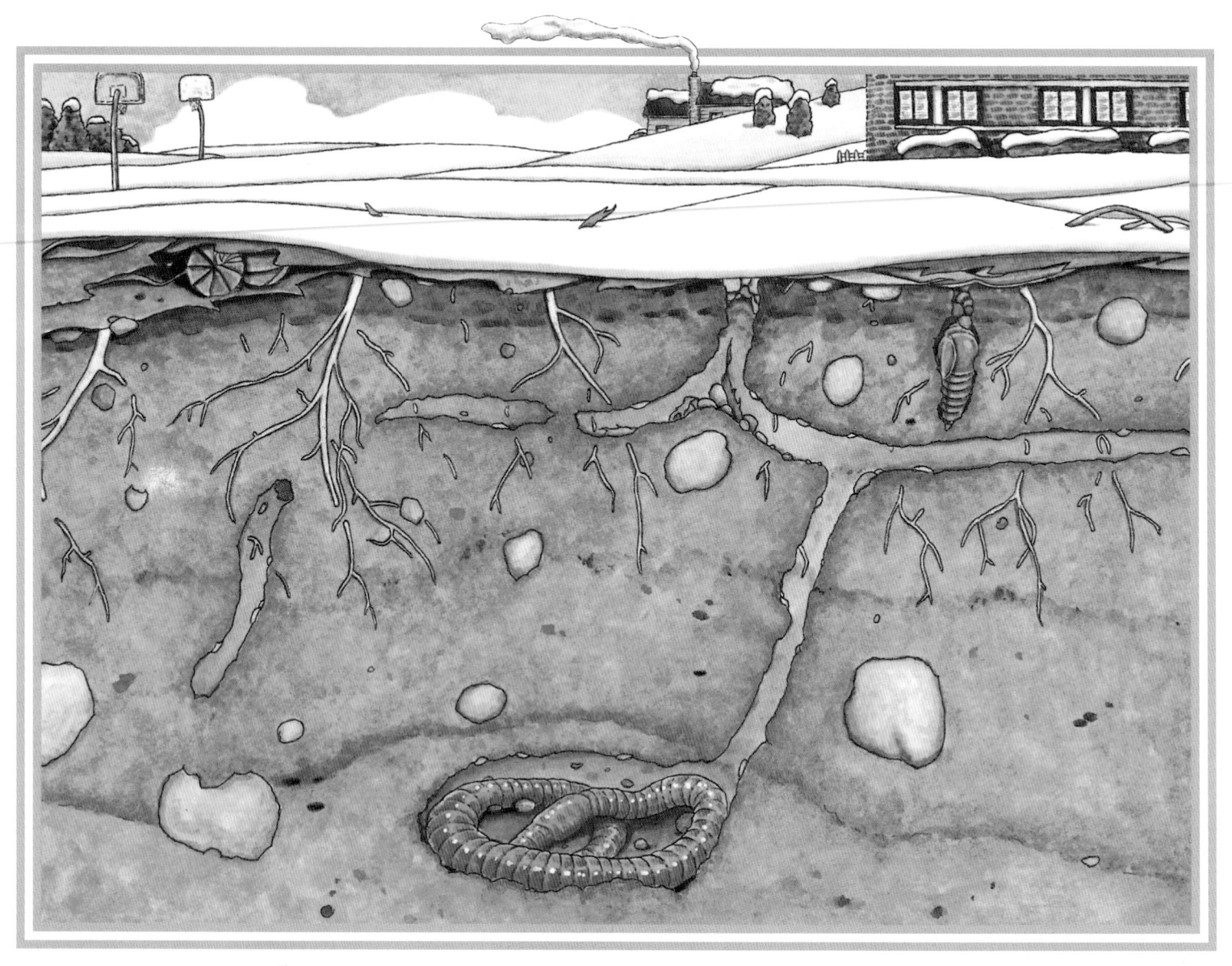

The earthworm eats the plants until winter. Then it is time to sleep.

Spring rains bring the earthworm back to the surface.

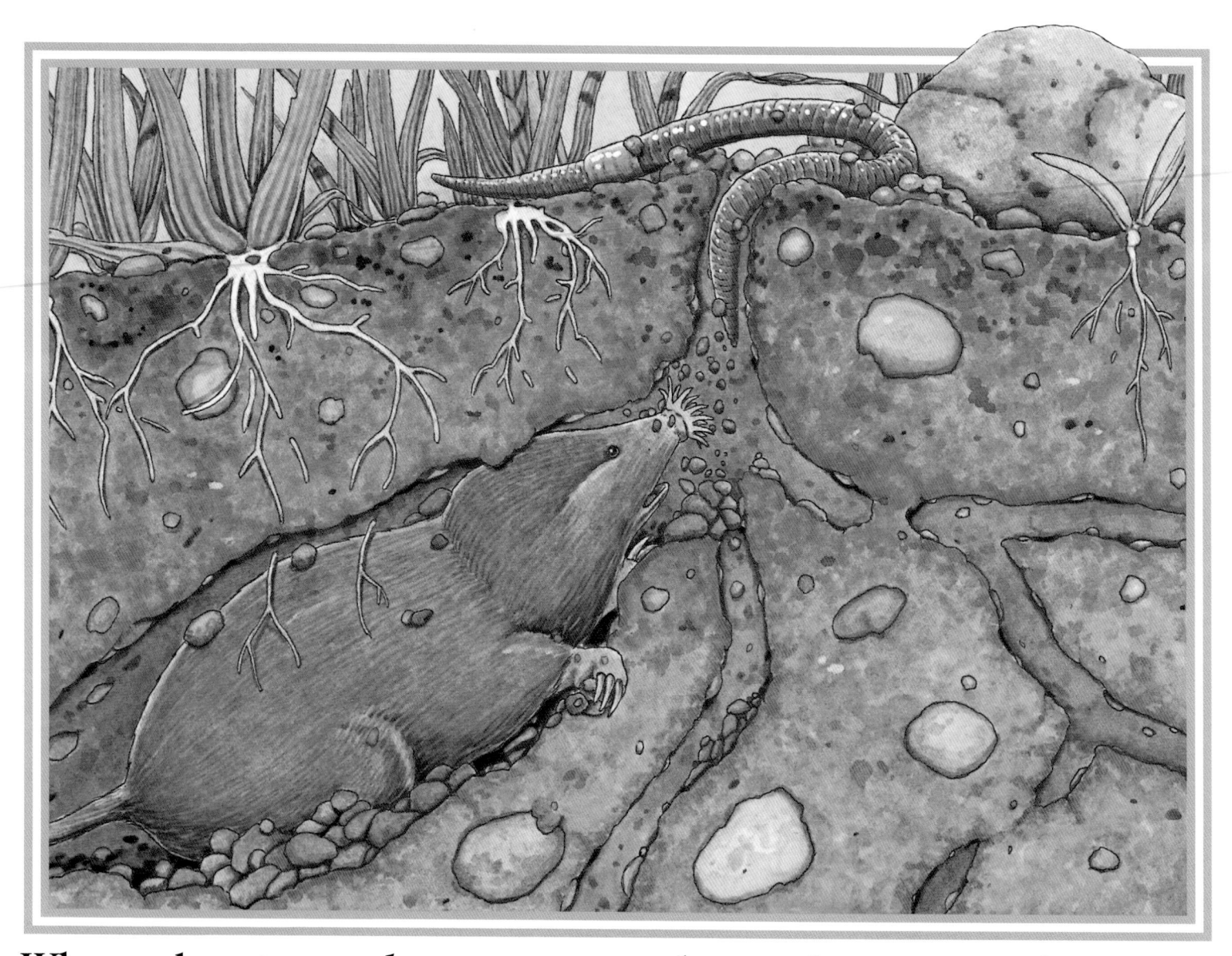

When a hungry *mole* comes near, the earthworm sneaks away.

The earthworm begins to look for a mate.

It finds one outside a nearby burrow.

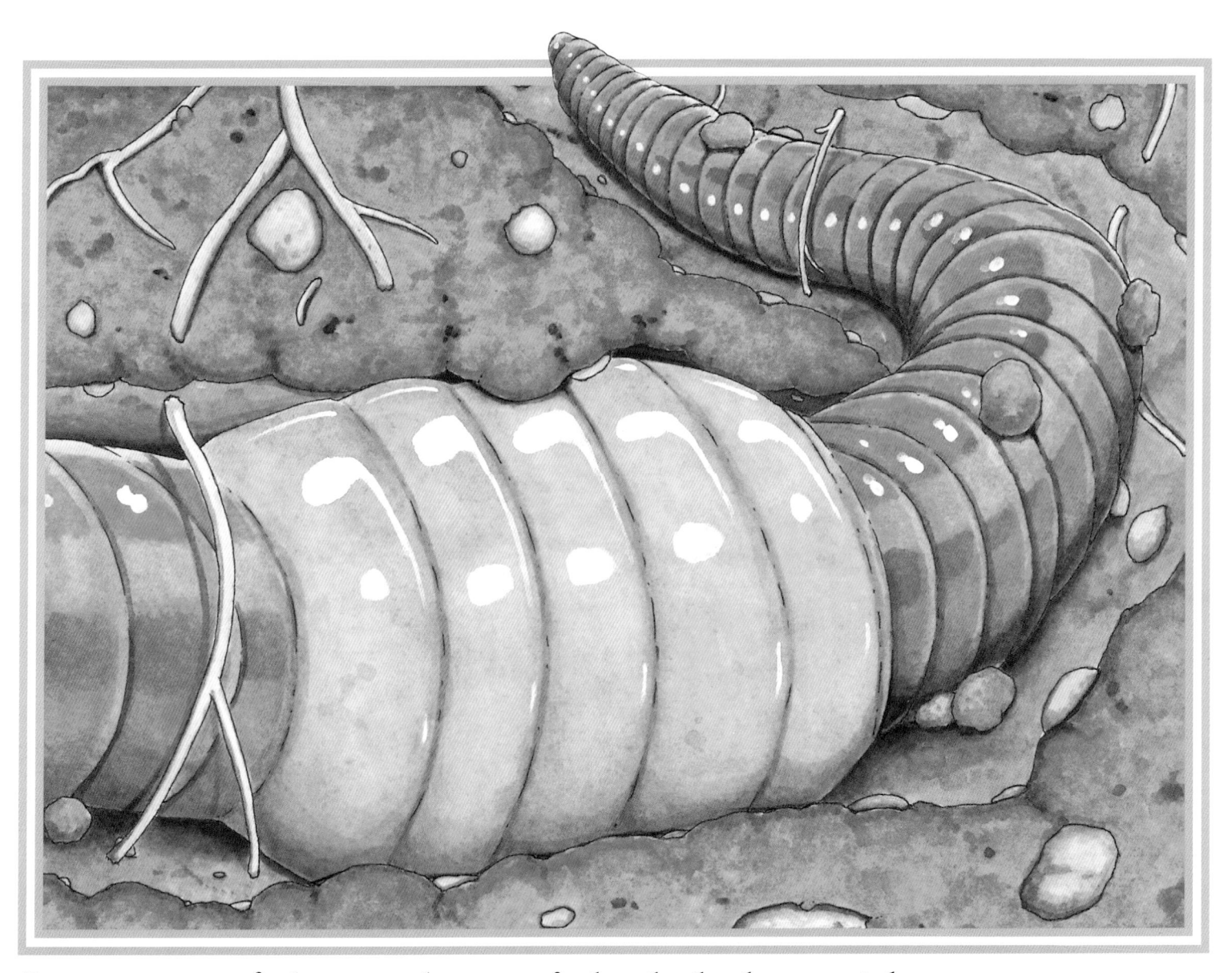

Soon, part of the earthworm's body bulges with eggs.

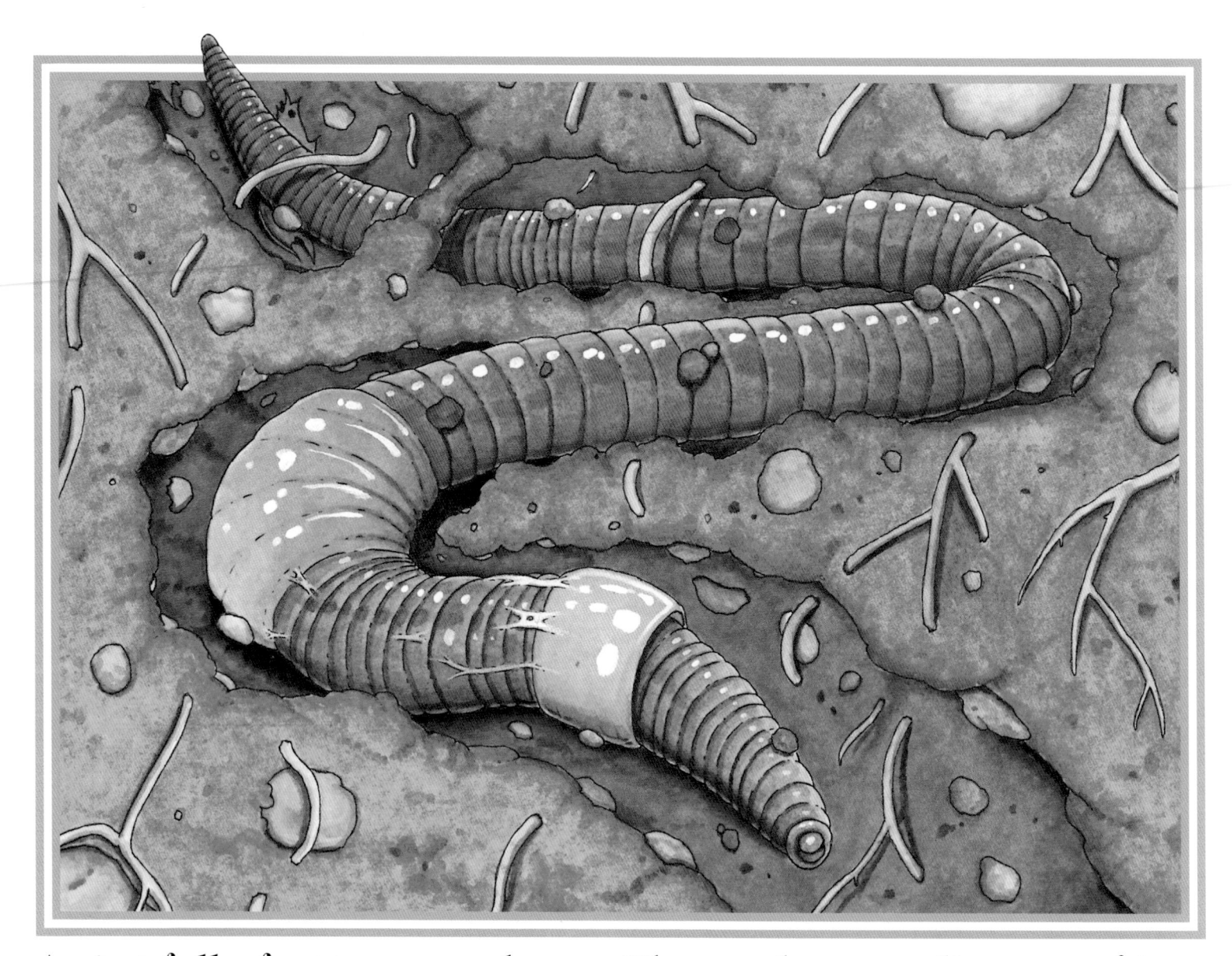

A ring full of eggs comes loose. The earthworm slips out of it.

The ring becomes an egg case. The earthworm leaves it behind.

When the earthworm comes aboveground, a *robin* grabs it!

The robin struggles to pull the earthworm out of its tunnel.

But the earthworm is strong. The robin gives up.

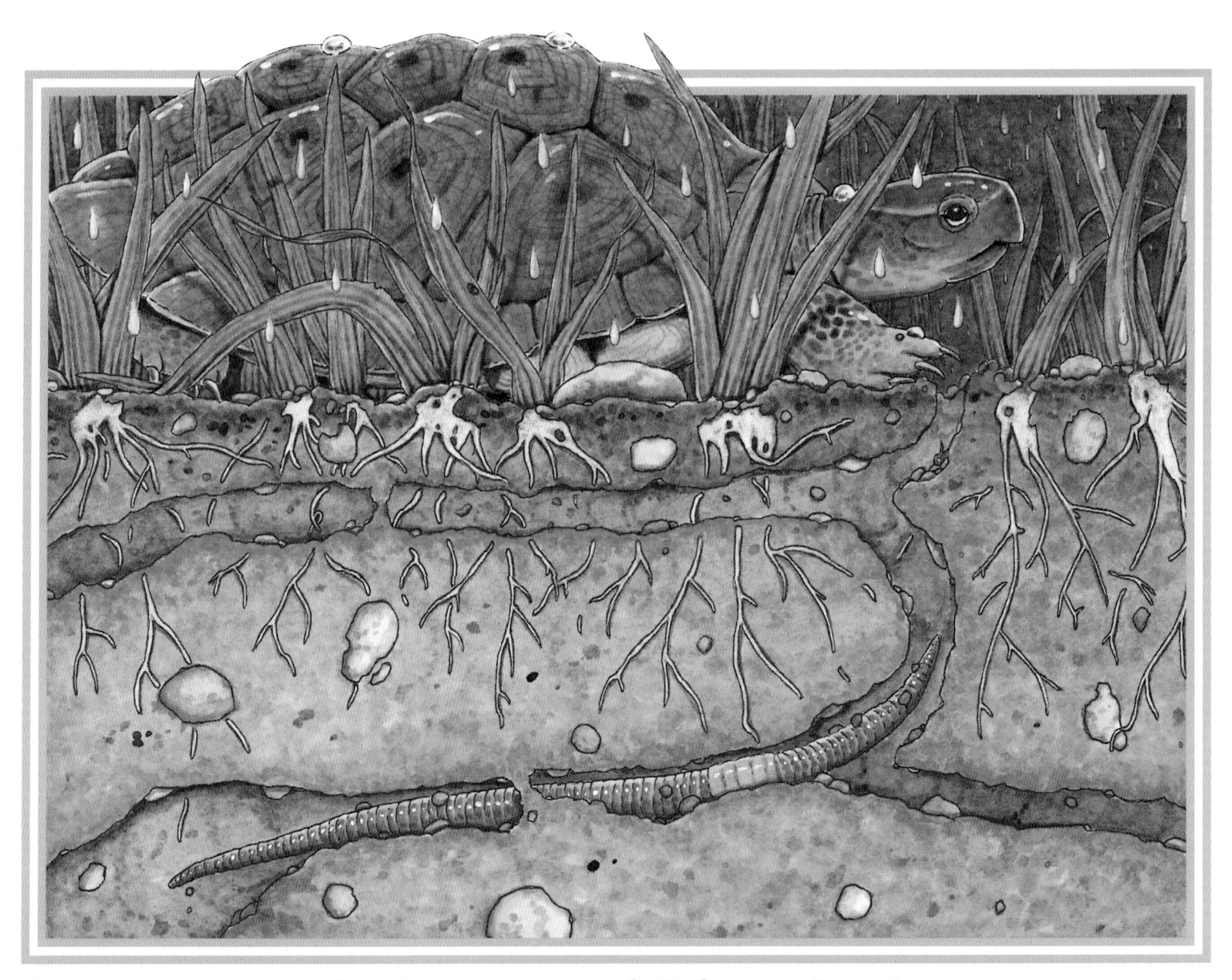

One summer night, heavy rains fall from the sky.

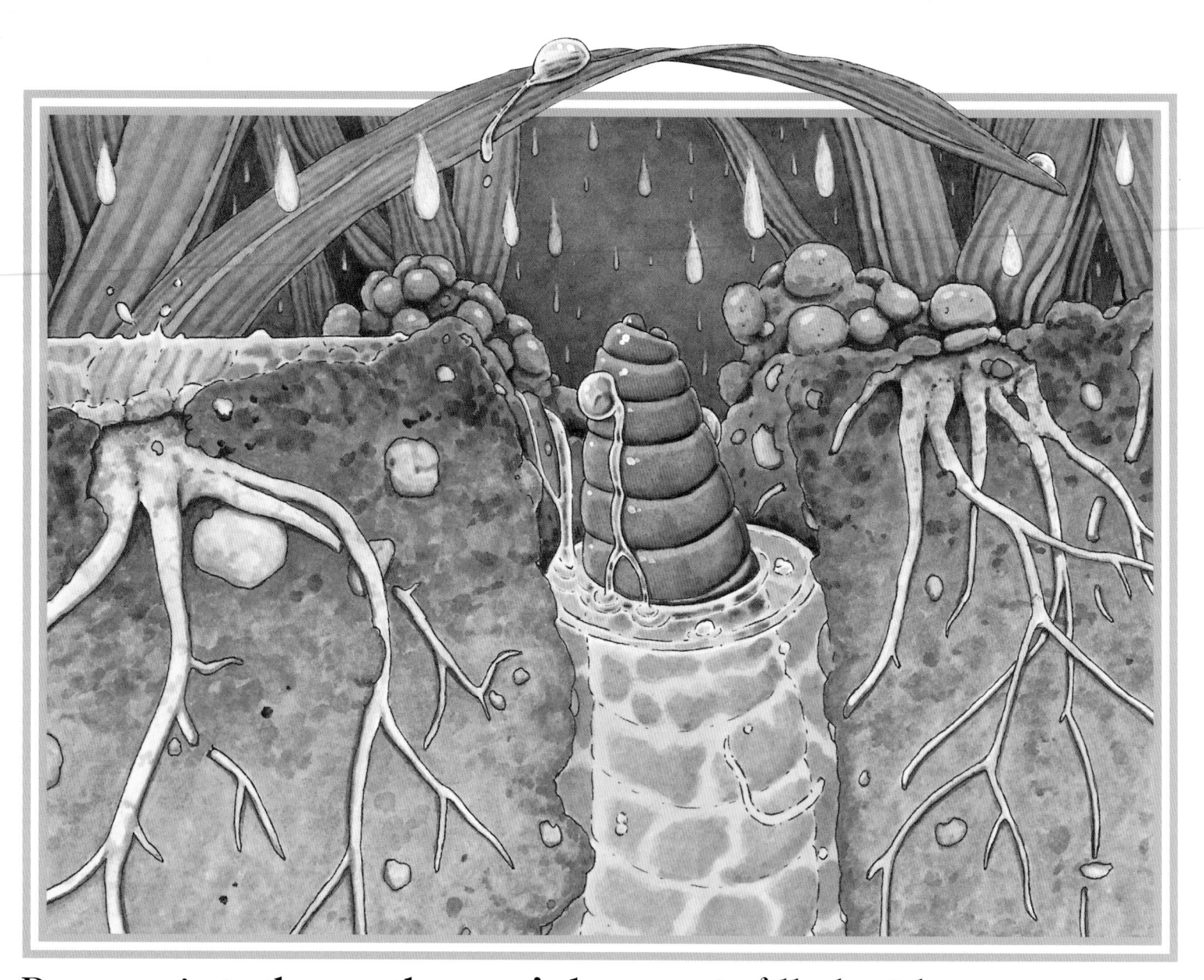

By morning, the earthworm's burrow is filled with water.

It searches for a drier place to live. But it gets stranded on a basketball court.

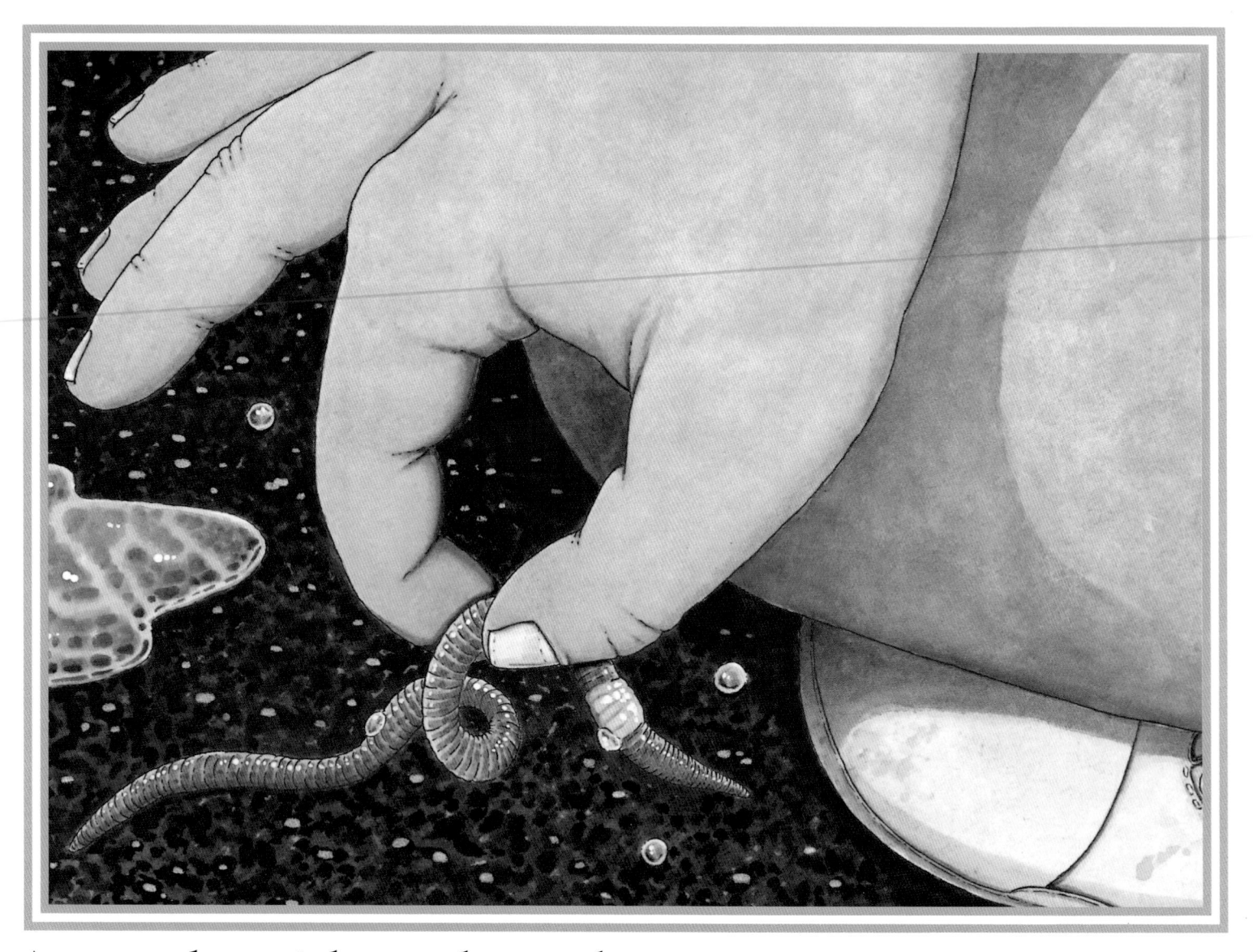

A young boy picks up the earthworm.

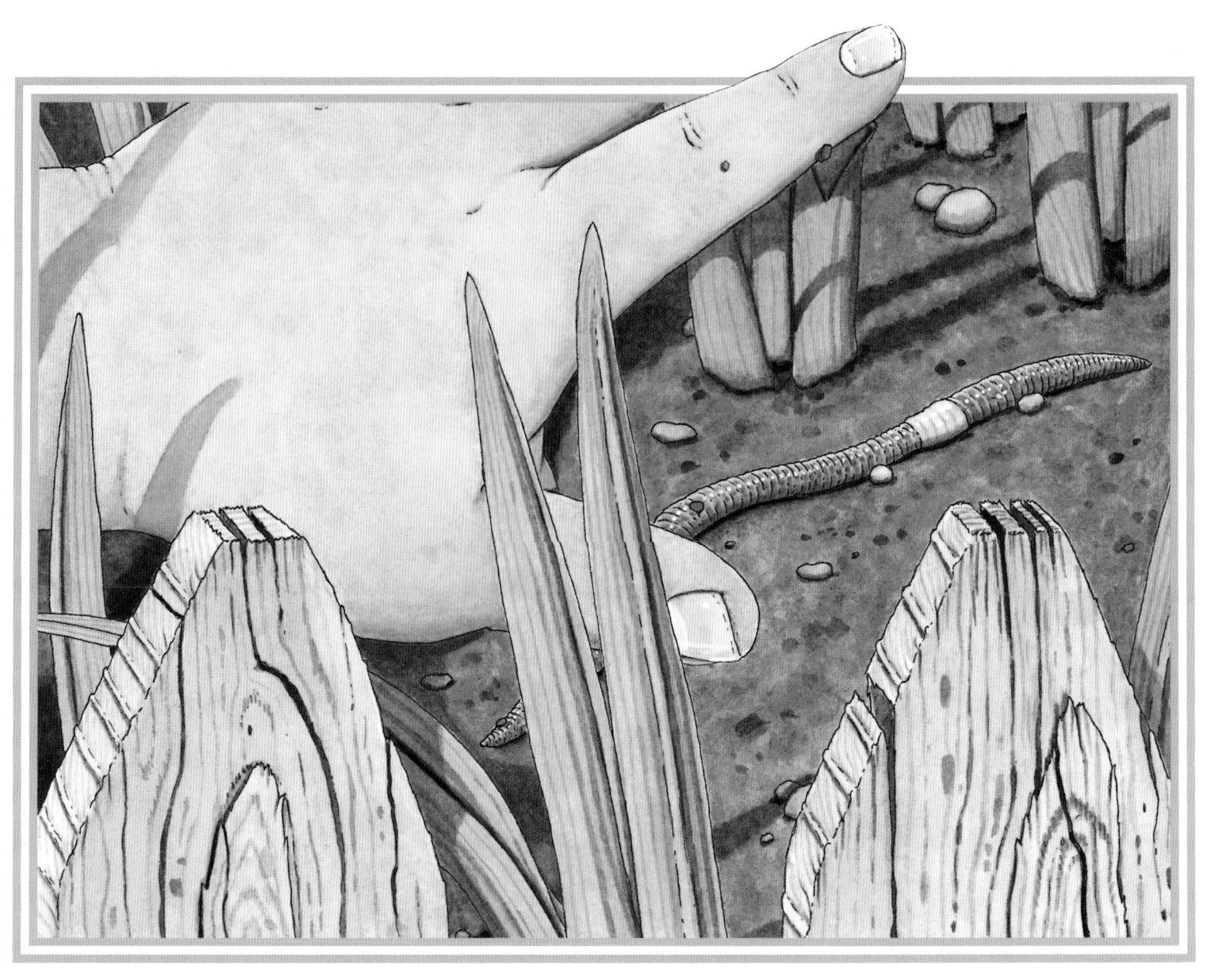

He puts it in a garden.

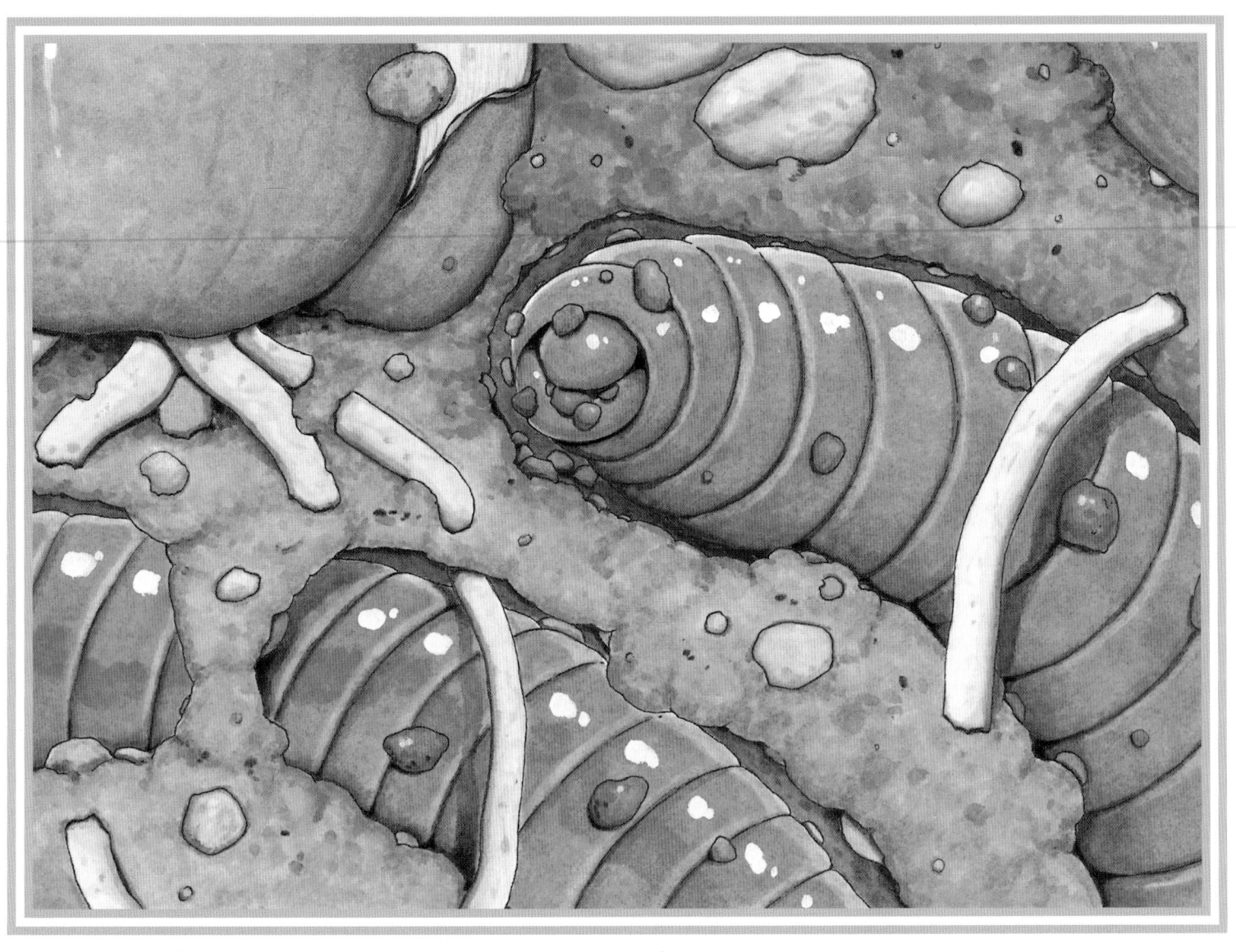

The earthworm spends the rest of the summer tunneling among *roots* and eating soil.

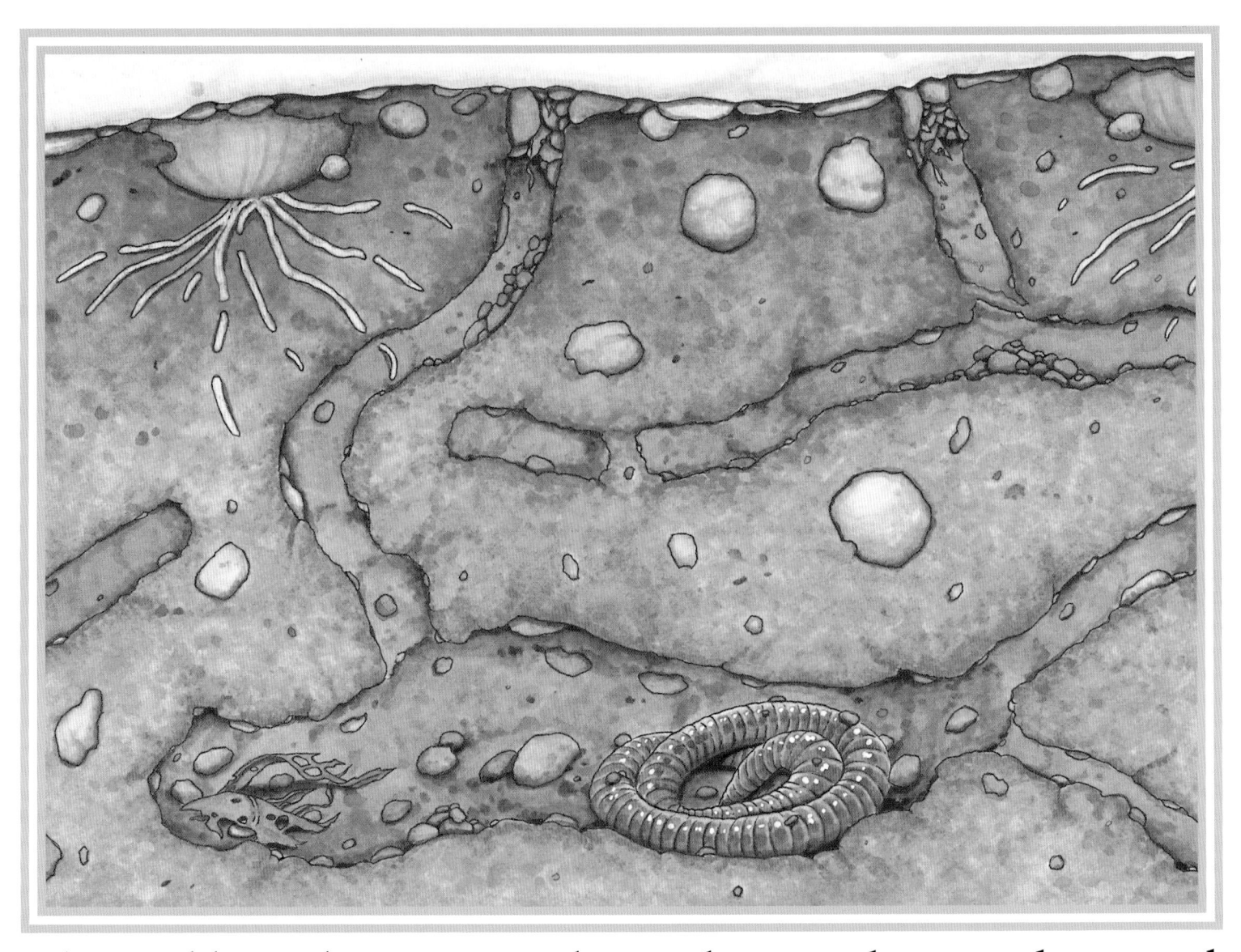

When cold weather returns, the earthworm sleeps underground.

In spring, the earthworm begins a new journey.

Words You Know

burrow—an underground tunnel

castings—piles of soil and plants that have passed through an earthworm

egg case—a protective covering for eggs

mole—a small mammal that lives underground and eats plants, insects, and earthworms

robin—a songbird that eats earthworms and insects

roots—the part of a plant that takes in water and nutrients from the soil. The roots of most plant grow underground.

soil—the upper layer of Earth that contains broken down rocks and rotting plants

About the Author

John Himmelman has written or illustrated more than fifty books for children, including *Ibis: A True Whale Story*, *Wanted: Perfect Parents*, and *J.J. Versus the Babysitter*. His books have received honors such as Pick of the List, Book of the Month, JLG Selection, and the ABC Award. He is also a naturalist who enjoys turning over dead logs, crawling through grass, kneeling over puddles, and gazing at the sky. His greatest joy is sharing these experiences with others. John lives in Killingworth, Connecticut, with his wife, Betsy, who is an art teacher. They have two children, Jeff and Liz.